Rob and Mom

by Kristin Cashore
illustrated by Bob Masheris

Scott Foresman
is an imprint of

Glenview, Illinois • Boston, Massachusetts • Mesa, Arizona
Shoreview, Minnesota • Upper Saddle River, New Jersey

Every effort has been made to secure permission and provide appropriate credit for photographic material. The publisher deeply regrets any omission and pledges to correct errors called to its attention in subsequent editions.

Unless otherwise acknowledged, all photographs are the property of Pearson.

Photo locations denoted as follows: Top (T), Center (C), Bottom (B), Left (L), Right (R), Background (Bkgd)

Illustrations by Robert Masheris

Photograph 8 Digital Vision

ISBN 13: 978-0-328-39290-2
ISBN 10: 0-328-39290-1

1 2 3 4 5 6 7 8 9 10 V010 17 16 15 14 13 12 11 10 09 08

Rob and Mom

use little rags.

Rob and Mom
use little pails.

Rob and Socks
use little rocks.

Rob and Mom use blue soap.

Mom drives from the barn.
Rob and Socks help.

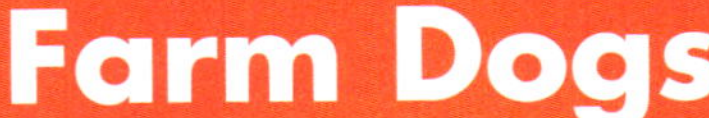

Farm Dogs

Read Together

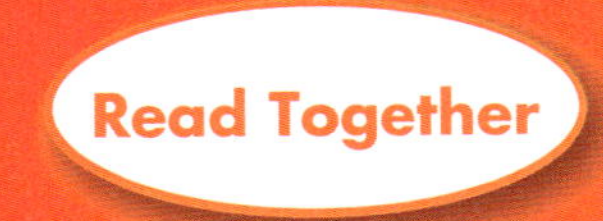

Farm dogs do not have much time to play in the mud! Farm dogs have many jobs. They help the farmer herd the animals. They keep the animals safe from wolves and foxes. They stop animals from eating the crops. Farm dogs are hard workers!

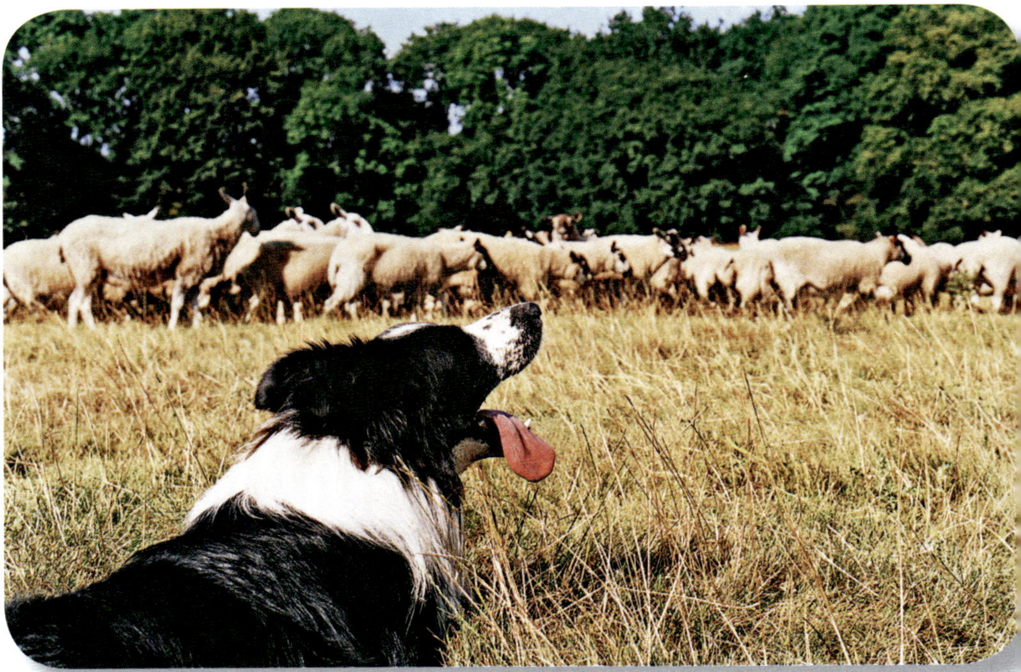